HOWL of the LAMBERGOON

Gad the Zig, Book 1

by Anthony Spaeth

illustrated by Marta Stawska

MFT
press

www.meatfortea.com

MFT Press

Easthampton, MA

First Edition, Second Printing

ISBN-10: 0-9975298-2-2
ISBN-13: 978-0-9975298-2-1
Howl of the Lambergoon
Copyright © 2017 Anthony Spaeth

FOR CECIL

The Faroes

Flatnose's Hall

Orkney

Geatland >

Outer Hebrides

X Callanish

Skye

Scotland

Mull

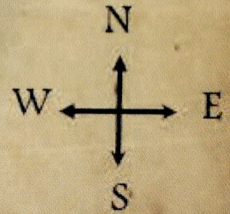

N

W — E

S

Howl of the Lambergoon

Gad the Zig, Book 1

I.   *The Forest Run*

In the Hebrides, in the olden days,

When Flatnose ruled the sea,

A servant boy called Gad the zig

Gathered clams by Loch Buie.

He'd a wee pony with him,

A Shetland he'd named Lull,

And she walked beside him to the sea

Where it washed the Isle of Mull.

They combed the beach all morning,

Then paused to sift their sack.

"Stay close now, Lully-girl," called Gad,

"We'll soon be headed back."

The shadows grew beneath them.

The wind turned out to sea.

The sun fell down the sky

To where the boiling waves must be.

Gad harnessed Lull again

And turned toward his master's home.

He led her in the shallows

To hide her hoofprints in the foam.

They came upon a narrow beach,
A place called Fenodrees' Dune,
And that's where Gad first saw it:
The fork-tongued lambergoon.

The creature had six crooked legs.

Its nostrils bled with slime.

Its eyes shone like silver plates.

Its scales were dark as wine.

As they watched, it glimpsed the moon
And spread its jaws out wide.
Its howl was like the winter wind.
"Ah-reeee! Ah-reeee!" it cried.

Lull's withers twitched with fear
And both her ears were bent.
"We'll take the forest path," Gad whispered,
"It's surely smelt our scent."

9

The woods grew near the shore there;

He pulled Lull toward the trail.

Her hooves sank in the loamy soil

While nettles grasped her tail.

The forest whirred with warnings:

Owls hooted in their hollows;

Crossbills sang out cerk-cerk-cerk

And toads croaked in their wallows.

The woodland path grew darker,
But they found nowhere to hide.
They heard the lambergoon behind them:
"Ah-reeee! Ah–reeee!" it cried.

And then, in an ambush by the trail,

They spied a ring-tailed tom.

The wily cat lurked in the shadows,

Watching, deadly calm.

Though the forest cat looked fierce,

Gad dashed on down the track.

"Don't bother over us!" he screamed,

"The lambergoon is back!"

After a few more strides,

Gad felt the sand beneath his feet.

The branches parted overhead

And he saw his master's keep.

And bless him! Bless him!
The old man was standing at his door!
He'd got his walking stick above his head;
He waved it and he swore!

"Run you fool!" the master shouted,
"The beast is in the wood!
Leave the nag behind, jug head,
Or be the demon's food!"

16

The forest's branches shuddered;

The goon sprang to the light.

Its teeth were wide and gnashing.

Its eyes were burning bright.

Lull whinnied—at the smell, at the sound,
At the beast now right behind—
She skittered on her rope;
She threw her head and whined.

Gad could not bear to look again;

Better not to know if he'd be swallowed.

He swatted the pony on her flank;

She bolted and he followed.

As they passed the master,

The old man stood to his full height.

He tapped his toe three times

And his cane burst into light.

A glowing eye gushed from his staff

And hung there in mid-air.

The lambergoon stopped short of it,

Trapped just beyond its stare.

The iris of the eye pulsed red
And then began to swirl;
It sucked back in the walking stick
Leaving just a smoky curl.

The master faced the snarling goon
As the last of his spell withdrew.
"Bring down that door!" he hissed,
"Before it knows I'm through!"

Gad turned the gate's pegged wheel
As the old man stepped inside.
The bars fell by the master's feet.
"Now blow that torch!" he cried.

Gad obeyed his master, as he must,

Snuffing out the only light,

But then he leaned toward the bars,

clicked his tongue –"thok" –

and whispered,

"No zig for you tonight."

The goon swung toward the gate,

Searching for Gad's face.

Its gaze was icy and hypnotic.

It froze the zig in place.

The monster crept upon him,

Inch by winding inch.

Gad felt its living heat

And smelt its rotten stench.

When, at last, it reached the bars,

It forced its snout inside,

And, leaning close to Gad . . . it spoke:

"Time will test your pride."

II. A Messenger from the Faroes

Some called the master "Hoon ga tree",

Meaning "One two three",

For he tripled every measure

No matter what it be.

29

Master Hoon knew several spells,

And some fair alchemy,

But what people came to him for most

They called his "Amnesty".

To drink the draught was to forget

And fall into a swoon.

When the patient woke again,

The world felt bright as noon.

Business was so brisk Hoon hid;

He disguised his keep like rocks.

Not every customer could find his gate;

Fewer still could work the locks.

But in the harvesttime,

Five days 'til summer's end,

A sail appeared upon the sea

And beat against the wind.

The skiff rounded ragged rocks,

Darting like a sparrow.

The captain jibed and tacked;

The way was hard and narrow.

When the pilot came into view

Wasn't Hoon surprised?

He nearly dropped his looking glass

And rubbed his rheumy eyes.

The helmsman was an island girl
With hair like a fiery brand.
She turned her ship toward shore
And beached it on the sand.

The woman seemed to know
The rock she was bound for:
She headed straight for Hoon's hide-out
Like a sign was on the door.

The old man raced down his steps

And slid into his lab.

By the time the visitor raised his gate,

He was grinding baobab.

Hoon glanced up at the woman, asking,

"You've a memory to free?"

But she cut him off quite curtly, saying,

"The king himself sent me."

"Call me Aud," she told him,

"I've a message from the Faroes:

A lambergoon is running wild there.

It's killed a jarl and all his fellows."

37

The islander took out her purse
And counted out six pence.
"This is to get rid of it," she said,
"Including travel and ingredients."

But Master Hoon was known to haggle
—Some thought him over-shrewd—
It would cost her a gold bar, he dickered,
Plus three pence for his food.

The bargain struck, Hoon rushed around,
Gathering all his things:
His spare robe and his pillow,
His willow wand and rings.

Gad packed the bogwood boxes
Filled with Hoon's apothecary,
Plus the wizard's tasseled carpet
And his glowing brambleberry.

Even Aud was asked to help:
Hoon gave her his grinding stones,
Then a bundle of dried roots
And a bag of broken bones.

By the time they left the tower,
All four were packed and stooped.
Aud pointed toward her tiny ship
Where its tattered sail now drooped.

But Hoon took out his carpet
And unrolled it on the sand.
He waived his wand and—one, two, three—
It rose to meet his hand.

The sly old wizard turned to Aud,
And, looking rather smug,
Said, "Leave your skiff at anchor, lass.
I only go by by rug."

So they took their seats and flew
With the stars and moon alight;
Hoon, Aud, Lull and Gad,
Whistling toward the Faroes
   —and the lambergoon—
     In the cool late summer's night.

III.   *The King in his Shattered Hall*

From the sky, the Faroes looked

Like mainly grass and sheep.

The mountains were all bald on top,

Snow-crowned and very steep.

When Hoon set his carpet down
Beside the king's great hall,
He found the village smashed to bits;
The goon had breached the wall.

Inside, Flatnose sat broken,

Sagging on his wooden throne.

His berserkers had deserted

And his men-at-arms had flown.

But Aud approached the king
And gave his sleeve a pull.
"Father, I found the wizard for you—
The Counting Mage of Mull."

Flatnose's eyes rolled to his guests;
He was deeply in his cups.
He slammed his fist and then he slurred,
"Kill that beast and all her pups!"

Just then the goon let out a howl
That shook the battered hall.
Flatnose staggered to the window
And swept his drapes back to the wall.

He pointed toward Mount Lokki
Where the beast brayed at the dawn,
"For seven years the creatures slept!
Seven years of calm!

"But Jarl Kraki! Jarl Kraki!
The great prince of the Geats
Showed up with his golden targe
In search of daring feats!

"And now I'm king of no one;
My army's fled the field.
Kraki woke the goons and ruined me!
Curse Kraki and his shield!"

Aud held a finger to her lips
And glanced aside at Hoon.
The magician got his kettles out
And his alabaster spoon.

He crushed three Ravens' Bills,
And mixed three Curds with Ambergris,
Then dripped three drops of Evening Dew
On the Cropstones of three geese.

The master boiled the motley mash
'Til it gave an orange light.
He held his glass aloft and swirled
To check his brew was right.

Finally, Hoon poured a dose
Of his famously forgetful draught;
Flatnose yanked the flask and guzzled it,
Fell to the ground and laughed.

Once the king was snoring,
The wizard walked around the hall,
Examining the hundred trophies
That were hanging on the wall:

There was a polished narwhal's tusk,
And a wrinkled walrus pelt,
An old bear's padded paws,
And a glinting sharktooth belt.

Also seven sealskins,
And the bills of six sawfish;
A tortoise shell big as a boat—
Each scale like a crockery dish.

Among the trophies, Hoon stopped at one:

A claw both thick and dire.

He touched its gleaming tip and asked,

"If she's pups, then where's the sire?"

Aud knelt beside her father,

Then slowly dipped her head.

"Kraki killed the bull," she whispered,

"But now that hero's dead."

Hoon took down the razor claw
And snapped it from its plaque.
He handed it to Gad, saying,
"Get your saddle and your pack."

The four of them left Flatnose sleeping
And headed for Mount Lokki.
As Hoon's rug rose, the she-goon howled:
She moaned, "Ah-reee! Ah-reee!"

IV.   *Den of the Beast*

By the time they reached the mountain,
The goon had disappeared.
Hoon set his magic carpet down
And stroked his ragged beard.

He picked a path along the ridge,
Searching rocky walls.
The way was steep and perilous
With loose scree and dead falls.

Lull was first to catch the scent—
The reeking of the dead.
They found a cavern stained with blood
Where the lambergoon had fed.

Hoon puzzled at the entrance,
Too low for him to stand.
He knelt as if to crawl;
Gad stayed him with his hand.

The master squinted at his zig
And beneath his breath cursed;
He made a single nod,
But gave this warning first:

"Be mindful of the goon, lad.
The beast's heart is likely sick.
Careful with that mouth of yours
And with the words you pick."

Hoon drew a dose of Amnesty
And pressed it in Gad's palm.
Gad took the pony by her lead;
He cooed to keep her calm.

But Aud was first to enter;
She pressed her way past Hoon,
Then ducked into the stinking cave
And headed for the goon.

The cavern wound and twisted,
Skirting ink-black pools.
They picked their way through dripstones
Shaped like ghasts and ghouls.

At last they saw a flicker
At the mountain's very core.
Gad pointed toward the faint light there
And soon made out a door.

The passage opened to a den
Where the beast lay on her side.
Her brood was sprawled around her;
Some suckled and some cried.

The goon's eyes shone on Gad.
Her forked tongue flicked its course.
"I've sssmelt you before," she lisped,
"The slave who wouldn't leave the horse."

Then she turned her gaze to Aud.
"And you brought the princess, too?
I've a message for your father, girl.
Tell him I'm not half through."

Gad didn't dare to speak,
But took the talon from his pack.
He held it where the beast could see;
The lambergoon reeled back.

"You bring me this?" she shrieked.
"You're more foolish than you look!
More brainless than that imbecile,
The jarl whose shield I took."

The monster pointed toward the wall,
Where Kraki's buckler hung.
"Perhaps you'd like to join him.
I've a spot there for your tongue."

"We're n-not here to show it,"
Stuttered Gad, with his hands shaking.
"We've brought it back to you,
To end the trophy-taking."

He raised the vial the master'd given
And uncorked the boll of cotton.
"This is Old Hoon's Amnesty," he said,
"Drink and pain's forgotten."

The lambergoon craned her neck,
Sniffing at the potion.
She closed her eyes and slowly smiled,
"How ssssoooothing is the notion."

But then he eyed her heartmate's talon,
Raking claws across the ceiling.
Gad watched as the sparks dropped.
The very stone was peeling.

"Put your medicine away," she snarled,
"My memories of my mate befit him.
They cost me dear to keep, that's true,
But it's still worse to forget him."

65

Then the goon's eyes slowly turned
To her squirming, mewling litter.
"Enough of pride
    and war
      and death,"
        she muttered,
"The more vengeance, the more bitter.

"I'll strike a truce with Flatnose
When he calls Mount Lokki mine;
He must plant a sign upon the slope
And warn his people not to climb."

Gad thought of Flatnose, dozing,
Having drunk away his memory.
They hadn't the right to bind the king . . .
But who was there to disagree?

It was Aud who stepped up, saying,
"I'm here in father's place.
Flatnose's war with you is done.
The mountain's yours down to its base."

The princess raised her hand in pledge,
And gave an oath upon her life.
The beast took down the shield and vowed,
"So we end the strife."

But as the goon returned her trophy,
She sobbed once, then recovered.
"Please . . . bury my lover's nail
Where it can never be discovered."

Aud took the golden shield
And Gad swore it would be so.
They each bowed to the beast,
Then left her to her woe.

So, children, the truce was made,
And it's held until today;
The goon's kept to her cave,
Though her brood's all swum away.

And Princess Aud, who made the peace,
Kept her solemn word.
She hammered in the sign herself:
"For the Lambergoon—Reserved."

"But where's the claw?" you ask;
I can tell you this and this is true:
Gad kept its resting place a secret,
As forgotten as Hoon's brew.

But if one day you reach the Faroes,
And there you visit Kraki's tomb,
Remember the zig who dug his grave . . .

And howl for the lambergoon.

71